A Kid's Guide to Drawing America™

How to Draw
Idaho's
Sights and Symbols

Jennifer Quasha

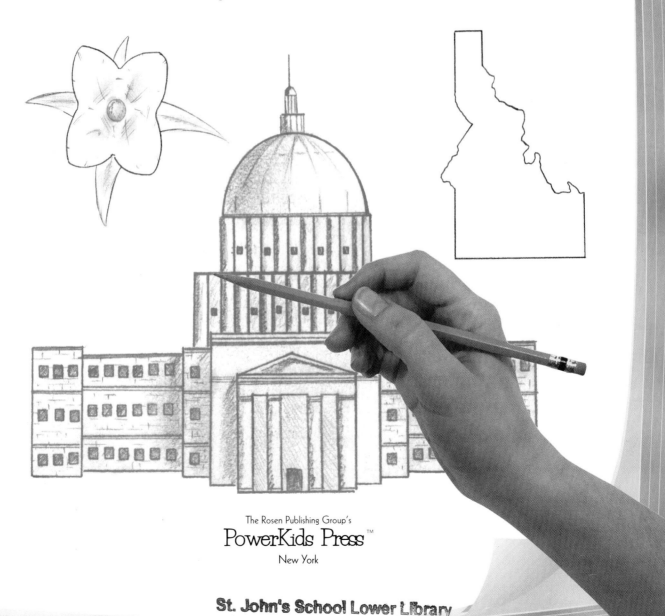

The Rosen Publishing Group's
PowerKids Press™
New York

Published in 2002 by The Rosen Publishing Group, Inc.
29 East 21st Street, New York, NY 10010

First Edition

Book and Layout Design: Kim Sonsky
Project Editors: Jannell Khu, Jennifer Landau

Illustration Credits: p. 18 Emily Muschinske; all other illustrations by Jamie Grecco.
Photo Credits: p. 7 © David Muench/CORBIS; p. 8 © (photo) Napoleon Sarony, from the Collection of Gilcrease Museum, Tulsa; p. 9 © (painting) Thomas Moran, *Shoshone Falls of Snake River* c.1900, Oil on canvas, 0126.2339, from the Collection of Gilcrease Museum; pp. 12, 14 © One Mile Up, Incorporated;
p. 16 © Hulton-Deuthsch Collection/CORBIS; pp. 18, 20 © Index Stock; p. 22 © Kevin Fleming/CORBIS;
p. 24 courtesy of the City of Pocatello; p. 26 © Kevin R. Morris/CORBIS; p. 28 © Dave G. Houser/CORBIS.

Quasha, Jennifer.
        How to draw Idaho's sights and symbols/Jennifer Quasha.
            p. cm. — (A kid's guide to drawing America)
        Includes index.
        Summary: This book describes how to draw some of Idaho's sights and symbols, including the state's seal, the state's flag, Cataldo Mission, and others.
        ISBN 0-8239-6068-4
        1. Emblems, State—Idaho—Juvenile literature   2. Idaho in art—Juvenile literature   3.
Drawing—Technique—Juvenile literature   [1. Emblems, State—Idaho   2. Idaho   3. Drawing—Technique]
I. Title   II. Series
        2001
        743' .8'09796—dc21

Manufactured in the United States of America

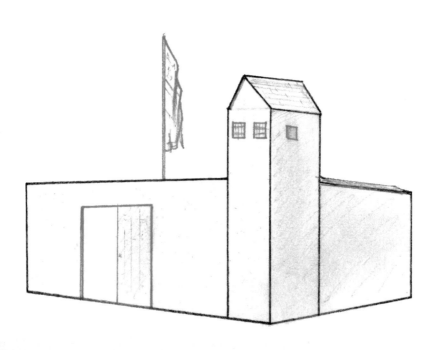

CONTENTS

Let's Draw Idaho

Idaho is a nature lover's paradise, with stunning scenery, terrific fishing, hiking trails, and wildlife like buffalo and elk. Three-quarters of all the people in Idaho live within 30 miles (48 km) of the Snake River, which runs across the southern part of the state. The Snake River flows past the world's richest Pliocene-epoch fossil bed, the Hagerman Fossil Beds National Monument. More than five million years ago, a lake covered this area. The soft lake floor preserved the remains of more than 200 Hagerman horses, close relatives of the modern zebra. Today the area is studied by scientists and is a popular tourist attraction.

Idaho is certainly known for its potatoes, but that's not all that's grown there. Dairy products, cattle, wheat, alfalfa, hay, sugar beets, barley, and trout are also part of Idaho's rich agriculture. Idaho has many industries, too, including tourism, food processing, forest materials, mining, chemicals, and production of electronics and computer equipment.

Idaho offers plenty of great subjects for budding artists, too. In this book, you will learn how to draw

Idaho's highlights. The drawing terms introduced below will help you as you go along. There are easy-to-follow steps that use basic shapes to help you get started and build from there. A red line shows each new step in the step-by-step illustrations, so you'll be drawing Idaho's sights and symbols in no time!

The supplies you will need to draw Idaho's sights and symbols are:

- A sketch pad
- An eraser
- A number 2 pencil
- A pencil sharpener

These are some of the shapes and drawing terms you need to know to draw Idaho's sights and symbols:

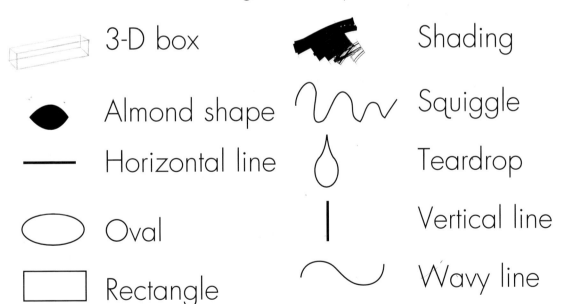

3-D box

Shading

Almond shape

Squiggle

Horizontal line

Teardrop

Oval

Vertical line

Rectangle

Wavy line

The Gem of the Mountains

On July 3, 1890, Idaho became the 43rd state to join the United States. About 1,300,000 people live in Idaho. Boise is Idaho's capital city, and its most populated city. More than 150,000 people live in Boise. People once thought that the name Idaho came from a Native American word for "gem of the mountains," but it does not. Idaho is a made-up word! Idaho has two nicknames, the Gem State and the Gem of the Mountains. This is because some of Idaho's mountains contain gemstones and precious metals. Idaho covers 83,574 square miles (216,456 sq km) and is home to the Clearwater Mountains, Salmon River Mountains, and Rocky Mountains, the Bitterroot Range, and other beautiful sights. Idaho also has Hell's Canyon, the deepest gorge in the United States at 7,900 feet (2,408 m) deep. In the 1960s, Craters of the Moon National Monument, which resembles the landscape on the moon, was used as a training ground for the astronauts of the Apollo 14 space mission team.

The lava beds shown here were named a national monument in 1924 by President Calvin Coolidge.

Artist in Idaho

Thomas Moran

Thomas Moran was born in Bolton, England, in 1837. His family moved to Philadelphia, Pennsylvania, in 1844, when Moran was seven. Unlike most artists of his time, Moran did not receive formal training in painting or drawing. As a teenager, he worked as an apprentice to a wood engraver in Philadelphia, and then in the mid-1860s, he and one of his brothers went to England to see the paintings of J. M. W. Turner, a famous landscape painter. Moran learned how to paint light and color by studying Turner's paintings. In 1871, Moran was invited to go with a geologist on a trip to the Grand Canyon and the Yellowstone River. Henry Jackson, a photographer, was also on the trip. Working together, the two men made such beautiful photographs and paintings of what was called the Yellowstone Territory that, in 1872, Congress was convinced by their artwork to make the area a national park. Moran became very famous for his paintings of Yellowstone, so much so that he began to sign his paintings Tom "Yellowstone" Moran. He worked in other mediums, including oils, watercolors, charcoal sketches, and pen-and-ink drawings. Moran died in Santa Barbara, California, in 1926.

In 1900, Moran painted *Shoshone Falls on the Snake River*. The painting measures 71 x 132 feet (22 x 40 m).

Map of Idaho

Map of the Continental United States

Idaho is a northwestern state and borders the states of Montana, Wyoming, Utah, Nevada, Oregon, and Washington, and the country of Canada. Idaho has seven regions, northern, north central, central, southwestern, south central, southeastern, and eastern. The state's highest point is Borah Peak at 12,662 feet (3,859 m). Idaho's several national forests include Boise, Clearwater, and Salmon-Challis. Many rivers flow through Idaho, such as the famous Snake River. There are dozens of lakes, including Lake Pend Oreille and Grays Lake. Idaho has a rich Native American culture and is home to Indian reservations such as the Coeur d'Alene, Nez Percé, and Fort Hall.

1

Draw a rectangle. This shape is a guide to draw in the state of Idaho. Draw the rectangle lightly so that you can erase the extra lines later.

2

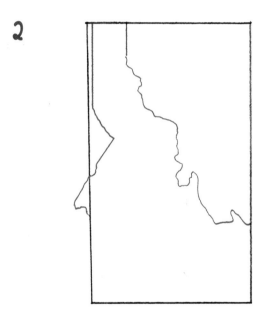

Use the rectangle as a guide and draw the shape of Idaho as shown.

3

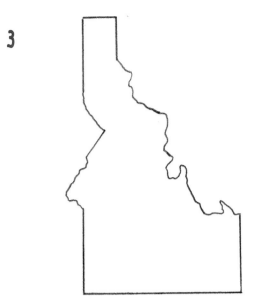

Erase any extra lines. Great job!

4

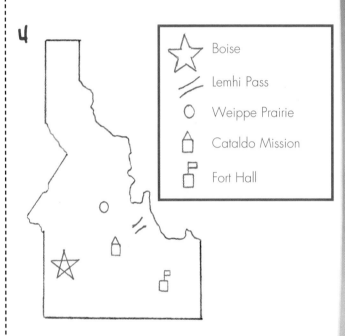

a. Draw a circle to mark Weippe Prairie.
b. Add two parallel lines for Lemhi Pass.
c. Draw a square. Then draw a triangle on top of the square. This is the Cataldo Mission.
d. Draw a square and a flag shape for Fort Hall.
e. Draw a star to stand for Idaho's capital, Boise.

The State Seal

The Great Seal of Idaho was officially accepted as the state seal in 1891, eight months after Idaho became a state. The seal was designed by Emma Edwards Green. She was the daughter of John C. Edwards, the governor of Missouri from 1844 to 1848. Emma fell in love with Idaho and its natural beauty during a summer visit in 1890. That year the state government held a contest for people to come up with a seal design for Idaho. When Emma's design was chosen, she became the first, and, so far, the only woman to design an American state seal! In 1957, the state legislature revised the seal. Now the official state seal is a painting by Paul B. Evans, based on Emma Green's design.

1

To begin lightly draw a large rectangle.

2

Next add a triangle as shown.

3

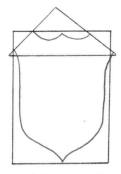

Draw the shape of the shield as shown.

4

Erase the extra lines. On top of the shield, draw two triangles for the elk. Draw a triangle in the shield at the right, for the tree.

5

Draw the elk's face as shown.

6

Erase the extra lines and draw the elk's antlers. Draw in the elk's nose and mouth.

7

Study the red guides carefully and draw the mountains, the clouds, and the river. Good job!

8

Add shading to your seal and erase any smudges. You are done!

The State Flag

Idaho's state flag was adopted in 1907. The background is blue and the state seal is centered on the flag. Under the seal, "State of Idaho" is written in gold block letters. In the seal, at the left, a woman holds scales and represents Justice. She also holds a spear with a liberty cap on top, representing Liberty. At the right is a male miner who stands for Idaho's important mining industry. The woman's position next to the man represents women's equality with men. The shield shows a pine tree, mountains, a river, and a farmer. The wheat sheaf and two cornucopias under the shield stand for Idaho's agricultural wealth. The head of an elk, a protected animal, rises above the shield.

1

Draw a large rectangle for the flag's field. Add a rectangle inside it that shares one wall.

2

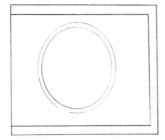

Then add two large circles in the center.

3

Draw two small ovals for the figures' heads.

4

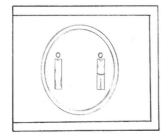

Add two rectangles, as shown, to help you draw the bodies inside the inner circle.

5

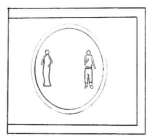

Erase any extra lines. Add arms to the man and the woman, and feet to the man.

6

Then add two triangles for the baskets and a rectangle for the wheat. Draw the woman's feet. You also can add a spear, a pick, and a shovel to the figures, using straight lines.

7

Look at the Idaho seal to learn to draw the elk and shield. Try to add the shapes shown here.

8

Erase any extra lines and add detail and shading to your flag. Under the circles you can write the words "State of Idaho."

The Syringa

The syringa *(Philadelphus lewisii)* became Idaho's state flower in 1931. *Lewisii* comes from the explorer of the West named Meriwether Lewis. He was part of the famous Lewis and Clark expedition. Lewis found the syringa flower in 1806.

The syringa also is called the mock orange flower because it smells and looks like the orange flower. It has a white, four-petaled blossom and grows in clusters at the ends of shrub branches. The syringa can be found throughout the northern part of the state. It is rare in the southern region. Native Americans loved the syringa. From the shrub branches, they made bows, arrows, baby cradles, and pipes for smoking. They even used its leaves to make soap!

1

Start by drawing a circle for the center of the flower.

2

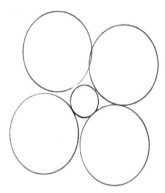

Next add four circles around the center. Try not to let them overlap.

3

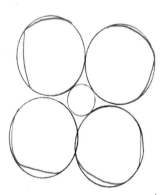

Draw the shape of the petals in the circles, as shown.

4

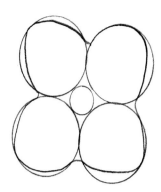

Connect the circles.

5

Add triangle-shaped leaves. Then erase any extra lines from the petals.

6

Add shading and detail to your flower. Erase any extra smudges. You've just drawn the syringa!

17

The Western White Pine

The western white pine (*Pinus monticola*) became Idaho's state tree in 1935. The western white pine is a large tree with blue-green needles that are from 2 to 4 inches (5 to 10 cm) long. There are five needles in every bundle. The tree's bark is thin and gray, and it becomes scaly as the tree grows. Its yellow-brown pinecones are from 5 to 12 inches (13 to 30 cm) long. The western white pine, native to Idaho and the Pacific Northwest, is often called by other names, including the Idaho white pine, mountain pine, and little sugar pine. Western white pines live for about 500 years and grow from 90 to 180 feet (27 to 55 m) high.

1

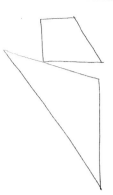

First draw the triangle shape and then draw the square-looking shape on top of it.

2

Use the triangle as a guide and carefully draw the tree trunk and the outline of what will be the tree branches.

3

Draw the tree branches. Notice how the tree trunk looks like it has three fingers.

4

Then draw the highest branch, which reaches way past the top of the tree trunk.

5

For smaller tree branches and twigs, draw small wavy lines on the big tree branches. Notice how they fork out in different directions.

6

For the tree leaves, draw a fluffy outline over the small branches and twigs. Shade the trunk.

7

Add detail and then shade the leafy areas of the tree. Erase any extra smudges and lines. You're done!

The Mountain Bluebird

The mountain bluebird became Idaho's state bird in 1931. Mountain bluebirds are about 6 ½ inches (17 cm) long. A male mountain bluebird is a rich blue color, although his head, chest, and sides are paler than the rest of his body. His underbelly is white and his tail feathers have white tips. Females are usually gray, although some are blue or greenish in color. Their throats and breasts are gray and their underbellies are white. The tops of the female's tail feathers are gray and the undersides are bright blue. They build their nests in holes in trees. Both female and male bluebirds take care of their broods and feed them insects, such as ants and beetles.

1

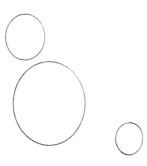

Start by drawing three circles for the bird's head and body. The largest circle will be the mountain bluebird's body.

2

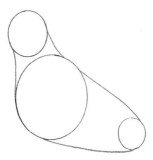

Then connect the circles with curved lines as shown.

3

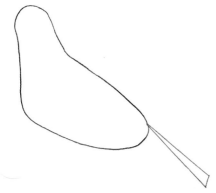

Erase any extra lines and add a triangle for the tail.

4

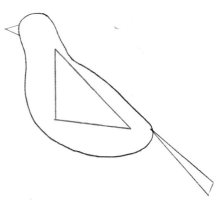

Draw two triangles, a small one for the beak and a big one for the wing.

5

Add lines for the bird's legs and feet.

6

To finish your mountain bluebird, add detail and shading. You can use your finger to smudge the pencil lines.

The Idaho Potato

Idaho produces more potatoes than does any other state in the United States. An Idaho potato is any potato grown in Idaho. Idaho potatoes include russet burbank, norkotah, and ranger russet potatoes. The first man to grow potatoes in Idaho was Henry Harmon Spalding, a Presbyterian missionary who established a mission in northern Idaho near Lapwai in 1836. He planted potatoes on a 15-acre (6-ha) plot of land to help the local Nez Percé Indians grow food. Ever since then, Idaho farmers have grown potato crops. Idaho's volcanic soil and the melting snow from its mountains help to irrigate the potatoes. These special conditions make Idaho an ideal place to grow potatoes.

1

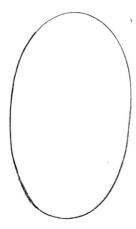

To draw your Idaho potato, start by making an oval.

2

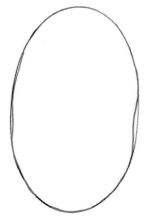

Next draw the shape of the potato in the oval, as shown.

3

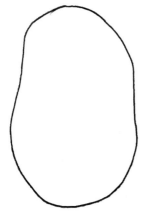

Erase any extra lines.

4

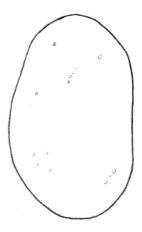

Add small circles in the potato for its spots, called eyes, which are buds.

5

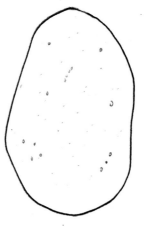

Use the tip of your pencil to draw dots on the potato for texture.

6

Add shading and detail to your potato. Erase any extra smudges. You're done!

Fort Hall

Fort Hall was one of the first permanent settlements in Idaho. It was established in 1834, by the Hudson's Bay Company from London, England. This company greatly aided the growth of the Pacific Northwest section of the United States. Hudson's Bay Company created trading outposts and rest stops for explorers as they traveled west. Fort Hall became an important outpost on the Oregon Trail. This is a trail that started in Independence, Missouri, and that ended in Willamette Valley, Oregon. Thousands of pioneers traveled westward on this trail. In Idaho, the Oregon Trail crosses the beautiful Snake River. Today a replica of the first Fort Hall stands in Pocatello, Idaho. Visitors can tour the restored outpost, which includes a log house, drugstore, and saloon.

1

Start by drawing three vertical lines, a long one near the center and two shorter lines on each side.

2

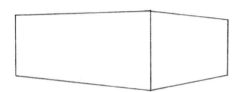

Next connect the lines.

3

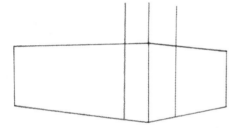

Add three more vertical lines.

4

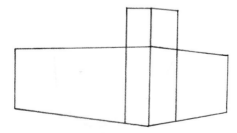

Connect the lines to form two rectangles on top of the building.

5

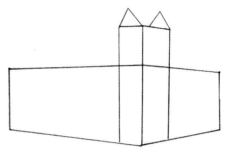

Add two triangles to form the roof of Fort Hall.

6

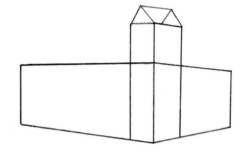

Connect the two triangles.

7

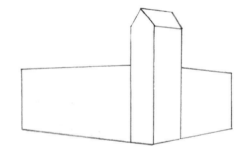

Erase extra lines and smudges.

8

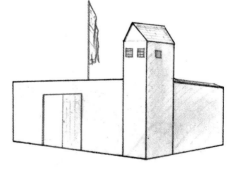

Add shading and detail to Fort Hall. You can also use rectangles to draw doors and windows. Add the shape as shown for the flag and flagpole.
You did it!

Cataldo Mission

The Mission of the Sacred Heart, located 24 miles (39 km) east of Coeur d'Alene in Cataldo, Idaho, is the oldest building in the state. Founded by Jesuits in the 1840s, it was designed by Friar Ravalli, an Italian missionary, and it was completed in 1853. His Greek Revival design came from the cathedrals of Europe. The Cataldo mission was built by Catholic missionaries and Coeur d'Alene Native Americans. It was built with logs from the area and was made with simple tools like axes, ropes, pulleys, and knives. Grass and mud were caked on top of the wood for more protection. The Jesuits decorated the mission with whatever they had, including chandeliers made of tin cans and wood painted to look like marble.

1

Start the Cataldo Mission by drawing a large rectangle.

2

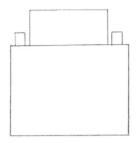

Then add three smaller rectangles on top of the first one. These will be part of the roof.

3

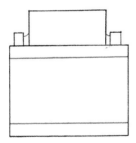

Connect the rectangles on the roof using slanted lines and add two long lines across the front of the mission.

4

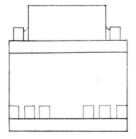

Draw six small rectangles to form the base of the columns. Notice how three are on one side and three are on the other side.

5

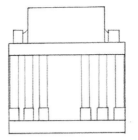

Add six thin rectangles on top of the smaller ones to form columns.

6

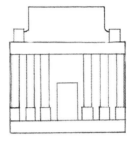

Erase any extra lines and add a rectangle in the center for the door.

7

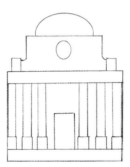

Add a half oval and a circle to the roof.

8

Add shading and detail to your building, like a cross on the roof. You can also draw rectangles for steps and for windows in the doors. You're done!

Idaho's Capitol

The Idaho state capitol building is located in Boise. A local building firm called J. E. Tourtellotte and Company began construction in 1906. From 1886 to 1912, the capitol was a red-brick building that stood near the site of the present capitol. Once the central part of the present capitol was finished in 1912, the government offices moved inside. The building firm became Tourtellotte and Hummel, and they built the east and west wings from 1919 to 1920. Most of the capitol is made of sandstone from an Idaho quarry called Table Rock. Idaho's capitol is the only capitol in the United States heated by geothermal water, which means the heat comes from hot water pumped from an underground source.

1

Start by drawing two large rectangles for the front of the capitol.

2

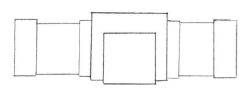

Then add six more rectangles. Notice their placement on the page.

3

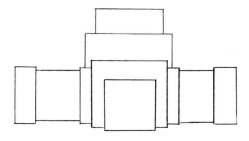

Draw two long rectangles on top of the middle of the building for the base of the dome.

4

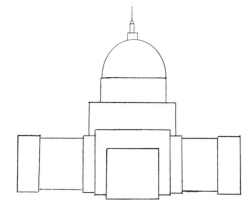

Add a large half circle to form the dome. Add two more rectangles on top of the dome. Next draw a second, small half circle and a long, thin rectangle to finish the peak of the dome.

5

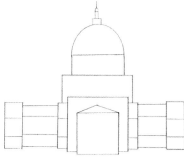

Add a triangle to the middle rectangle as shown. Draw lines across each building.

6

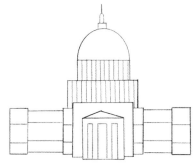

Using thin rectangles, add columns to the building, including the top.

7

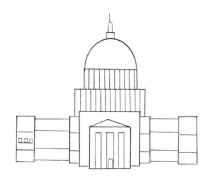

Draw in all the windows and doors by adding small squares as shown.

8

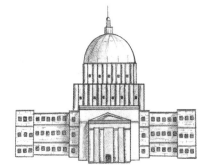

Add shading and detail to your capitol building. Erase any extra smudges. You just drew Idaho's capitol!

Idaho State Facts

Statehood	July 3, 1890, 43rd state
Area	83,574 square miles (216,456 sq km)
Population	1,251,700
Capital	Boise, population, 152,700
Most Populated City	Boise
Industries	Food processing, forest materials, mining, chemicals, production of electronics and computer equipment
Agriculture	Potatoes, dairy products, cattle, wheat, alfalfa, hay, sugar beets, barley, trout
Tree	Western white pine
Bird	Mountain bluebird
Flower	Syringa
Fish	Cutthroat trout
Gemstone	Star garnet
Horse	Appaloosa
Insect	Monarch butterfly
Song	"Here We Have Idaho"
Dance	Square dance
Nicknames	The Gem State, the Gem of the Mountains
Motto	*Esto perpetua* (It Is Forever)

Glossary

apprentice (uh-PREN-tis) A person who learns a trade by learning from a skilled craftsperson.

broods (BROODZ) Young birds hatched from eggs at the same time.

cathedrals (kuh-THEE-druhlz) Large churches that are run by bishops.

chandeliers (shan-duh-LEERZ) Lighting fixtures that are hung from the ceiling.

cornucopias (kor-nuh-KOH-pee-uhz) Curved goats' horns that often hold fruit and ears of grain. Cornucopias signify abundance, or having a lot.

expedition (ek-spuh-DIH-shun) A journey made for a particular reason.

geologist (jee-AH-luh-jihst) A scientist who studies the structure of the earth.

geothermal (gee-oh-THUR-muhl) Something that relates to Earth's core.

gorge (GORJ) A steep, narrow passage through land.

irrigate (EAR-ih-gayt) To supply land with water through ditches or pipes.

Jesuits (JEH-zoo-itz) Members of a Roman Catholic Society founded in 1534.

legislature (LEH-jihs-lay-cher) A body of persons that has the power to make or pass laws.

mission (MIH-shun) A place where religious leaders teach their religion.

missionaries (MIH-shuh–nehr-eez) Religious leaders who go to a country to teach their religion.

mock (MAHK) Fake.

outposts (OWT-pohsts) A frontier settlement, such as a fort.

Pliocene-epoch (PLY-eh-seen EH-pihk) A period of geological time from 5.2 to 1.6 million years ago.

Presbyterian (pres-bih-TEER-ee-un) A branch of the Christian religion based on the teachings of Jesus Christ.

preserved (prih-ZURVD) To have kept something from being lost.

reservations (reh-zer-VAY-shunz) Areas of land set aside by the government for Native Americans to live on.

space mission (SPAYS MIH-shun) An organized trip in a spacecraft.

Index

Web Sites

To learn more about Idaho, check out this Web site:
www.state.id.us